The Rooftop Races

The Rooftop Races

Toshesh Meena

First Edition – 2025
Published by **ADTC Creative Studio**

DEDICATION

"To everyone running their own race— may you find your own sky to soar, and a moment to catch your breath."

ACKNOWLEDGMENTS

First and foremost, thank you to the pigeons.

Not just the literal ones cooing from balconies and dodging ceiling fans—but the metaphorical ones too. The ones grinding, gliding, and occasionally crash-landing through the maze of modern life. You inspired this flight of poetry.

A warm thank you to all the friends, teachers, mentors, and unsuspecting fellow runners in this great rooftop race of exams, expectations, and existential dread—you made the journey chaotic, confusing, and oddly poetic.

To the ADTC Creative Studio crew (which may or may not just be me in a hoodie with too many tabs open)—thank you for the creative chaos and stubborn persistence to see this book through.

Lastly, to every reader who's ever felt like a bird in a storm, may these verses remind you that even in the race, there's still room to perch, ponder, and laugh.

Keep flying, even if you're not sure where the finish line is.

Toshesh Meena

ABOUT THE AUTHOR

Toshesh Meena has stumbled through the trials of Academia, Competitive grind, and Existential dread. From the trenches of school report cards to the labyrinth of civil services prep, he's run laps around syllabi, schedules, and sleep cycles.

When not navigating exam timetables or modern life's maze, he dabbles in poetry, storytelling, and curious metaphors involving pigeons. *The Rooftop Races* is his debut poetic collection—a satirical yet sincere reflection on ambition, anxiety, and the absurdity of it all.

He currently writes, creates, and occasionally get few things done under the creative banner of **ADTC Creative Studio**.

PREFACE

Let's get this out of the way: this is a book about pigeons.

Or at least, it pretends to be.

What you're actually holding is a metaphor in disguise — an allegorical journey through the trials of ambition, competition, and the modern rat race (except, well, with wings and feathers). These poems follow a flock of pigeons swept up in a mysterious, almost mythic "race." They don't know who started it or exactly what the prize is, but they join anyway. Because everyone else is doing it. Sound familiar? Whether you're a student buried under exam prep, a professional sprinting toward KPIs, or just a human trying to make sense of why you're always busy — these poems might hit home. Especially if you've ever thought, mid-crisis, "Wait, why am I even doing this?"

Originally inspired by the relentless and often absurd pressure cooker of academic competition — particularly the kind found in highly competitive exams — this series of poems expands into something more universal. The race may start in a classroom, but it doesn't end there. It creeps into careers, social status, online personas, and anywhere someone is trying to "get ahead" without always knowing who they're racing or why. This collection doesn't offer solutions. No self-help advice. No twelve-step plan. Just a flock of slightly confused, occasionally rebellious pigeons trying to navigate a world that told them to fly fast but never explained where to land. So whether you're reading this from a library, a living room, or a rooftop (pigeon optional), I invite you to enjoy the journey. And maybe — just maybe — take a moment to question your own race.

Feathers optional. Curiosity required.

Toshesh Meena

AUTHOR'S NOTE

I didn't start writing this book with pigeons in mind. But somehow, they became the perfect metaphor.

Like many others, I've spent a fair share of life racing. First, it was grades in school — the invisible leaderboard haunting every report card. Then came the college entrance exams, where you learn the true meaning of competition (and caffeine). And eventually, I found myself in the most elite gladiator arena of them all: the civil services examination. A multi-year epic of syllabi, rankings, expectations, and silent existential dread.

If you're reading this, there's a good chance you've been in a race too — maybe still are. Whether it's academic, professional, or one of those self-imposed marathons like "achieve something meaningful before 30," the feeling is universal.

The poems in this collection took shape during breaks — the rare pauses between laps. They're not self-help mantras or motivational chants. They're quiet reflections, dressed up as feathery allegories. Pigeons just made it easier to talk about ambition, pressure, herd mentality, and hope — without getting too heavy-handed.

This isn't a manual to escape the race. Honestly, I'm still in it myself. But perhaps, like me, you'll find some relief in naming the madness, in laughing at it a little, and in remembering that every now and then, it's okay to stop flying in circles.

Keep flying,

Toshesh Meena

CONTENTS

PART 1: THE LOFT'S ECHO

> "Hope whispers loudest before the race begins."

1

Whisper in Rafters

They heard it first in broken beams,
A whisper caught between the seams.
"A race is coming," soft and sly,
"A prize awaits beyond the sky."

The fledglings fluffed, the elders stirred,
A myth reborn from half spoke word.
"To soar, to shine, to beat the rest!"
"To leave the gutters, pass the test!"

Yet none asked why or who had said,
The sky held gold above their head.
For once a dream begins to gleam,
Few pause to question such a dream.

2

Dreamer Featherbright

Featherbright perched near the dawn,
Wide eyed, his sleep long gone.
"The race! The race!" he softly cried,
As if it flapped inside his pride.

"I'll fly so fast I'll blur the sky,
And kiss the stars while soaring by!"
He preened his wings with hopeful flair,
A champion born on morning air.

The others chuckled in the beams,
But Featherbright just chased his dreams.
For he believed, with all his might,
That sky-born wishes must be right.

3

Crumble the Cynic

Old Crumble scoffed from shadowed perch,
His feathers dull from years of search.
"I've seen a thousand races run,
And not a one has reached the sun."

"They talk of prizes, wings of fame,
But most just fall back where they came."
He eyed the hatchlings full of fire,
Then sighed, "They'll learn it's all a mire."

Yet still he watched, with squinted eye,
The hope that lit the morning sky.
And in that gaze, so dry and grim,
Flickered a spark long lost to him.

4

Peckman's Prep Talk

"Attention, flock! Line up, stay tight,
This race will separate wrong from right!"
Coach Peckman flapped and puffed his chest,
As if his squawk could bring out their best.

"Eat grit for breakfast, train your glide,
Build your stamina, stretch that stride!"
He scribbled plans in sunflower seed,
And taught ambition, trimmed of need.

"Your worth," he cried, "is what you chase,
Now flap, you slackers! Own this race!"
And though his talk was all technique,
Some pigeons wondered "What's the peak?"

5

Nestling No. Nine

Nestling Nine was far too small,
To grasp the meaning of it all.
She watched the bustle, heard the cheer,
But didn't feel the need to steer.

She waddled circles in the hay,
Then tried to lift, then chirped halfway.
"Will I race?" she asked her friend.
"Or stay behind and just pretend?"

No answer came, just loftlight gold,
That warmed her feathers, soft and old.
She cooed and sighed beneath the beam,
Not every bird must chase a dream.

6

Gossip

Three pigeons perched by broken slate,
Their claws curled close in idle wait.
"I heard the race decides your name"
"No, no, it grants eternal fame!"

"It's flown at dawn, or dusk... or both?"
"That's nonsense feather folk take oaths!"
They chirped and clucked and fluffed with pride,
Each lie inflated, none denied.

And in the nest below the eaves,
The younger ones clung to beliefs.
For even rumor, when it's bold,
Feels warmer than the loft when cold.

7

Number 43

He hatched the week the whispers came,
So no one thought to give a name.
Just "Forty Three," a scribbled mark,
Upon his wing, still faint and stark.

He listened close but asked no thing,
Just stared in silence, preened his wing.
For even pigeons learn to mute,
Their questions when the race is truth.

When others dreamed of clouds and speed,
He nested deep, ignored the creed.
But still his chest felt tight each night,
The quiet cost of not taking flight.

8

Loft Elders' Council

Three ancient birds with stoic eyes
Declared the race both "foolish" and "wise."
They'd flown it once when skies were war,
And earned their perch near roosting door.

"With every wingbeat, truth grew thin,"
Said one with rust along his chin.
"And yet," the second cooed aloud,
"It taught us how to dodge a crowd."

The third, with voice both cracked and slow,
Said, "Racing's flight, but flight ain't soul."
They nodded once, then shut their eyes,
And left the young to chase the skies.

9

Chalk on the Chimney

Someone had scrawled a shaky sign:
"WINNERS GET THE SKYLINE FINE"
No bird confessed to carving it,
But every head turned up a bit.

They circled 'round the words at dusk,
And muttered praise or called it "fluff."
But none erased the message there,
For dreams, like chalk, can cling to air.

Even Crumble, cold and dry,
Looked up with doubt behind his eye.
For in the race both cruel and kind,
Even lies can fuel the mind.

10

Sunrise Rehearsal

They gathered near the eastern spire,
And flapped in sync like wings on fire.
Not racing yet, but testing lift,
As if momentum was a gift.

They leapt from tiles with half-hopes pinned,
Then tumbled down in morning wind.
One clipped a wire, another fell,
But laughter rose and all was well.

They trained like children play pretend,
Convinced the wind would one day bend.
And though the sky was far and wide,
It felt like something real inside.

11

Wingtip Polisher

She polished wings with bits of glass,
Then checked reflections as they passed.
"If form is flight and flight is grace,
Then perfect feathers win the race."

She trimmed each quill, she smoothed each barb,
Her nest smelled faintly sweet and sharp.
Yet flying? Rarely done at all,
Her wings looked fast but feared the fall.

She taught the chicks to shine and gleam,
To chase not flight but loft esteem.
For in the race, she often said,
You win by how you turn your head.

12

Perch for Popular

A rooftop ridge became the stage,
Where winged pigeons preened with age.
They scoffed at drills and flapped askew,
Too proud to race, too sharp to lose.

One called the race "a myth for fools."
Another mocked the training rules.
Yet deep inside, their feathers twitched,
Each time a hatchling's gaze had switched.

They ruled the perch with tilted brows,
But sometimes stared at distant clouds.
The ones too proud to chase the sky,
Still watched it passing slowly by.

13

Loft Bell Rings

A bell! A bell! A clang! A peal!
The rumor screamed: *"It's getting real!"
The loft burst out in beating wings,
As if the bell confirmed all things.

"Tomorrow starts the pre-flight check!"
"Wait was that from the church, or deck?"
It didn't matter truth was sound,
And once it rang, the flock was bound.

Some cried. Some danced. Some looked around.
But no one dared to doubt the sound.
A single bell, and still they swore,
That they were born for something more.

14

Talon Ledger

A pigeon named Grey Mottled Finch,
Kept score of every training inch.
He logged each glide, each tumble-fall,
Each wingbeat made, both short and tall.

He wore his charts like second skin,
Obsessed with what he might not win.
And though his stats were quite elite,
He barely saw the world beneath.

He flew in loops no joy, no cheer,
Just numbers echoing his fear.
And every chart, no matter right,
Still failed to measure what felt light.

15

Nestside Goodbye

"My love," she said, "don't fly too far,
Just trace the curve below that star.
And when you find what lifts your soul,
Don't let the race become the goal."

But he was fluffed and chest held wide,
Determined not to stay inside.
He cooed a promise, half sincere,
Then kicked from slate and disappeared.

She stayed behind and cleaned the nest,
And watched the sun fall west by west.
A whisper echoed in the beams,
The race can cost the warmest dreams.

16

Who Didn't Sign Up

They passed her by with hurried pace,
Too slow, too still to join the race.
She'd shrugged when asked to "list her name,"
As if she couldn't feel the flame.

"I like the view," she softly said,
While scratching crumbs beside her head.
She'd seen the chalk, the charts, the drills,
But found no rush in chasing hills.

And so they scoffed and flapped away,
A non-racer? Who'd choose to stay?
Yet in her quiet, dusk came near,
And she flew loops with nothing to fear.

17

Ghostwing

He flew before the races grew,
Before the first prize banners flew.
No one had seen him since that day,
A whispered myth that fades away.

Some say he won and rose so high,
He pierced the fabric of the sky.
Others insist he lost and fell,
Where gutters gape and shadows dwell.

But still his name gets tossed like dust,
By birds who flap and dream and trust.
For in each race, some hope to find,
The ghost who left it all behind.

18

Slate-Tile Confession

A pigeon wept on broken slate,
And cursed the wings he learned too late.
"I wanted fame I thought I might...
But something's wrong with how I flight."

He wasn't slow. He wasn't weak.
He'd simply lost the need to seek.
The more he trained, the less he knew,
What drove him through the sky's wide blue.

He wrote his name in droppings dry.
Then watched the wind erase it shy.
And still he told no soul his doubt,
For fear the other's would throw him out.

19

Roof Itself Speaks

Beneath their claws, the roof let sighs,
Tired tiles beneath bright skies.
"I've borne your dreams and every fall,
I've caught your flights and every call."

"I've heard the chants and seen you break,
I've watched the truth behind the fake."
The pigeons never heard the groan,
Of rooftop bones worn down to stone.

But if they paused mid-preen or pose,
They'd hear a voice beneath their toes.
Not loud, not cruel, but simply wise,
A voice not meant for racing skies.

20

Feather Falls

It drifted down through loftlight slow,
A single plume let softly go.
No bird could say whose feather fell,
But somehow all had felt it well.

It danced on beams, then dropped from view,
A quiet end, a silent cue.
Was it from joy, or fear, or age?
Was it release, or just a stage?

They watched it fall, then looked away,
Too much to think, too much to say.
But somewhere deep in chest and claw,
They felt the flaw in what they saw.

21

Whispered Doubt

Amid the crowd, a whisper grew,
A subtle voice no one quite knew.
"Is this the path we truly seek,
Or just the race that makes us weak?"

But louder roars would drown the sound,
As wings beat fierce and hearts unbound.
Still, in the quiet, doubts persist,
A fragile flicker in the mist.

For even in the fastest flight,
A whispered doubt can spark the light.
That questions why we chase the sky,
And if the race is worth the try.

22

Hidden Strain

Beneath the feathers, muscles ache,
A hidden strain they all must take.
No one sees the silent toll,
The breaking points that crack the soul.

The crowd expects the endless glide,
But not the scars they try to hide.
Each wingbeat costs a price unknown,
A burden carried all alone.

Yet strength is forged in quiet pain,
And every fall is not in vain.
The hidden strain may break the bone,
But also teaches wings to own.

23

Fractured Trust

Among the flock, a rift was sown,
A fracture made, though seeds unknown.
Promises whispered, then withdrawn,
Trust broken in the fading dawn.

The race once shared by wing and heart,
Now split apart by fear and art.
Some chased glory's distant gleam,
While others lost the common dream.

But broken trust can heal with time,
And fractured wings can still climb.
For even when the bonds are bent,
New strength may rise from discontent.

24

Silent Pact

In secret shade, a pact was made,
A quiet vow beneath the glade.
To fly not just for fleeting prize,
But for the truth behind the skies.

No cheering crowd, no urgent call,
Just wings that rise beyond the wall.
A silent pact to seek the real,
The flight where hearts alone can heal.

Though others raced in frantic blur,
This pact would guide them far and sure.
For sometimes silence speaks the most,
A gentle flight away from ghosts.

25

Flicker Within

A single spark inside the chest,
A flicker fighting for its rest.
Though storms may rage and winds oppose,
That tiny flame still brightly glows.

It's not the prize nor cheers that feed,
But something deeper, quiet seed.
A hope that grows beyond the race,
A pulse that sets a steadier pace.

That flicker holds the strength to rise,
To break the chains and claim the skies.
For in the darkest, wildest spin,
There always burns a light within.

26

Feather Lottery

They drew their numbers from a sack,
Each feather dipped in inky black.
"This one," they said, "determines fate,
Your launch time and your flighting gate."

Some got dawn. Some dusk. Some none.
The rules were clear, except for one.
No bird quite knew who ran the draw,
Or why the feathers felt like law.

But still they clutched their chosen shade,
As if the sky were fair and made.
And even those who knew it flawed,
Still flapped in faith to please the fraud.

27

Mid-Beam Breakdown

A pigeon cracked at 2 a.m.,
Just muttering lines again and again.
"If wings don't win, then what are they?
If flight's a test, can I just stay?"

He stared into the half-moon's face,
And shook beneath his practiced grace.
The race had not yet even come,
But still his chest beat like a drum.

No one approached. No one said "pause."
They left him clinging to his flaws.
For fear, when seen, becomes a curse,
A flaw one hides, lest it get worse.

28

Polisher's Regret

She'd spent her life on shine and gloss,
On every plume and perfect cross.
But now she watched the fledglings spin
And wondered what she'd missed within.

"I taught them gleam. I sold them sky.
But never once said *why* to fly."
She stared at mirrors cracked by time
And mourned the weight of empty rhyme.

And still she polished every wing,
That begged to glitter, stretch, and cling.
For truth, once sold, is hard to mend,
Especially near a soaring end.

29

Sky's First Shadow

That morning brought a darker hue,
The sky looked off, a deeper blue.
The clouds were shaped like broken glass,
And winds moved strangely through the grass.

Some said, "It's weather, nothing more."
But others paused beside the door.
For even air can taste like fear,
When racing day is drawing near.

The sky, once promise, felt like test.
A looming dome above each nest.
And in that hush, a silence spread.
The kind you hear before you're led.

30

Sleep in the Loft

They curled in nests, some tight, some flat.
Some dreamed of gold, some dreamed of "that."
One murmured songs. One clenched claws.
One whispered, "Maybe break the laws."

A hush moved through the rafters slow,
A breath before the great unknown.
No chirps. No flaps. Just shallow sleep,
The stillness pigeons rarely keep.

And in the dark, the loft exhaled,
Its planks and bricks no longer veiled.
A world of birds, asleep and blind,
Still thinking flight would free the mind.

PART 2: THE ROOFTOP TEST

> "Preparation breeds chaos when the goal is unclear."

31

Morning Drill Madness

At dawn they leapt from ledge to ledge,
Flapping through their daily pledge.
"Faster, higher! Stretch your wings!
The prize awaits what training brings!"

But some just tumbled, feathers fried,
While others napped, exhausted, wide eyed.
No coach in sight, no guide, no plan,
Just frantic flapping wing to fan.

Yet still they rose with hope anew,
Though battered, bruised, unsure what to do.
For dreams can push through frantic fear,
A broken wing can still persevere.

32

Endless Circle

Round and round the rooftop went,
Chasing tails and time well spent.
"Keep circling! Don't stop now!
You'll make the flock so proud somehow."

But dizzy eyes began to blur,
And some just paused to ponder her.
The bird who laughed and didn't race,
Who watched the chaos with calm grace.

She whispered softly to the breeze,
"Sometimes to fly, you must find ease."
Not every path is straight and fast,
Some journeys cherish moments passed.

33

Advice Avalanche

"Flap low! Flap high! Flap in between!
Eat seeds! Don't eat! Be lean and mean!"
Every pigeon shouted "Try this way!"
And every bird's mind went astray.

Confused and frazzled, they complied,
Though no one really knew the guide.
Some copied each ridiculous tip,
While others lost their steady grip.

In endless noise, a truth was lost:
That silence often counts the most.
Within the chaos, find your beat,
Not every voice is meant to meet.

34

Wing Weight Fiasco

They strapped on weights, they strapped on bands,
Dreaming of stronger, faster hands.
But soon the wings began to tire,
And flight felt less like soaring fire.

One bird declared, "This is insane!"
While others begged to try again.
The weight grew heavy on each bone,
Yet still, no one flew on their own.

At last a whisper broke the strain,
"True strength is born through gentle gain."
No added weight can teach the skies,
But steady wings and patient tries.

35

Mid-Roof Injury Report

A pigeon limped with feather torn,
Another squawked, "I'm hardly born!"
The injuries stacked, the panic rose,
But no one dared to say, "It shows..."

The pain was masked by grit and pride,
Though many flapped with tears inside.
For in this race, to stop was shame,
A loss that carried no one's name.

Yet some hearts whispered, soft and low,
"That healing's part of how we grow."
To fly again, we must first mend,
And wounds can lead to brighter end.

36

Coach Who Couldn't

He squawked and shouted, feathers askew,
But never once took flight anew.
"Stretch! Sprint! Turn!" his calls rang clear,
Though none had seen him in the air.

His wings were clipped by some old tale,
Yet still he led the training trail.
The pigeons listened, tried their best,
While he just puffed his chest and guessed.

But deep inside, a silent pain,
A wish to soar beyond the chain.
A leader's heart can sometimes yearn,
For flights they never had the turn.

37

Wing-Twister Drill

They spun in circles, flapped and flipped,
Until the rooftop under slipped.
"Twist your wings! Now dive and dive!
This is how the best survive!"

Some lost balance, some lost beak,
Some lost days they'd never seek.
But no one dared to call it off,
For quitting meant they'd pay the scoff.

Yet in the dizzy, swirling fight,
A lesson hid beyond the flight:
Sometimes to find your way anew,
You must first lose your sense of true.

38

Seeds of Doubt

The feed was rationed, secrets kept,
Some birds ate while others wept.
"Only the chosen get the best,"
Whispered voices from the nest.

But hunger gnawed and spirits waned,
And some began to feel untrained.
For how to fly when hollow inside?
When trust was thin and hope had died?

Yet in the shadows, hope can sprout,
A hungry heart will find a route.
For even starving wings may rise,
When fueled by dreams beyond the skies.

39

Flashy Flyer's Fall

He zoomed and zoomed, a streak of light,
The loft's proclaimed "bright star" in flight.
But pride took hold and wings went wild,
He crashed beneath the rooftop's mild.

Feathers ruffled, dignity torn,
He hid away, ashamed, forlorn.
Yet soon he preened and called for more,
Eager to race and soar once more.

For every fall can teach the brave,
To rise beyond the crash and crave.
A fall's not end—it's just a part,
Of learning flight from heart to heart.

40

Whisper Network

Between the chimneys, secrets passed,
Advice and rumors flying fast.
"Don't trust the coach, avoid the weight,
Watch who's favored by the gate."

The pigeons formed their quiet clans,
To find some hope in others' plans.
But every whisper held a sting,
The race was more than just a wing.

In shadows deep, the truth is found,
That trust and doubt both circle 'round.
To fly ahead, the flock must learn,
When to unite and when to turn.

41

Overthinker's Flight

She flapped and flailed, mind tangled tight,
Calculating wind and light.
But thought too much, she stalled mid air,
Too frozen trapped to dare the dare.

Her wings beat rhythms out of sync,
While others soared on instinct's brink.
"Fly by feel," a quiet voice said,
But logic ruled inside her head.

Till finally she let it go,
Released the mind's relentless flow.
And found the sky was hers to claim,
Not thought, but heart, would win the game.

42

Group Push-Up

"Down! Down! Push hard!" the coach declared,
The pigeons dropped, their feathers bared.
One flapped, one gasped, one barely moved,
The rooftop echoed with their prove.

But some just crouched, worn thin and slow,
While others pushed beyond their glow.
The test was pain disguised as pride,
And none could stop the rising tide.

Yet strength is not just muscle's show,
It's knowing when to pause and grow.
For wings that push too far and fast,
May break before the race is past.

43

Lost Feather

A single plume drifted away,
Caught by a sudden gust astray.
It twirled and danced without a home,
A silent ghost through air and foam.

The flock glanced up, then looked away,
Too busy in the race's sway.
Yet in that lost and lonely fall,
Lay meaning deeper than them all.

For sometimes losing small and slight,
Can clear the path for clearer flight.
What seems like loss may just prepare,
A lighter heart can take the air.

44

Latecomer's Rush

He flapped in breathless, frantic pace,
Chasing a spot, a fleeting place.
"Wait up!" he cried, wings barely strong,
As others soared so swift and long.

But catching up was not so sweet,
When breath was gone and hearts did beat.
He learned the race was cruel and fast,
A game no late bird could outlast.

Still in the chase, he found a spark,
A lesson lit within the dark.
That sometimes rushing's not the way,
But steady wings can win the day.

45

Rooftop Roar

At dusk the loft erupted loud,
Cheering cries, a frantic crowd.
"Tomorrow's the day! Be ready now!"
Voices cracked with eager vow.

But underneath the raucous cheer,
Beat nerves masked well by eager sneer.
For every shout and every grin,
Hid fear of what would soon begin.

Yet in that night, a quiet peace,
A moment's calm, a soft release.
For dawn will come with wings anew,
And every heart must dare to do.

46

Feather Flexers

They preened and puffed, each plume displayed,
As if the race were just parade.
Flexing wings in sunlit gleam,
Showing off their polished dream.

But strength isn't in shining bright,
Nor in the gloss of morning light.
True power hides in silent flight,
Yet none could see beyond the fight.

One quiet bird, unseen, unsought,
Moved with strength that needed naught.
No need for show, no need to gleam,
Just steady wings and peaceful dream.

47

Strategy Session

Around the ledge, they whispered low,
Plans spun out, like wind would blow.
"Take the left! Avoid the crow!
Fly the gaps where breezes go."

But every scheme bred doubt anew,
Confusion thick as morning dew.
When no one knows what's real or true,
Every plan feels overdue.

In swirling doubts, a truth was lost:
The best laid plans can bear the cost.
Sometimes to win, you must let go,
And trust the wings that you well know.

48

Fatigue Dance

Feathers drooped and bodies swayed,
Some still ran though colors grayed.
Pushing past the break and bend,
Chasing dreams that wouldn't end.

But tired wings are fragile things,
Cracking under harshest stings.
And even flight can lose its wings,
When all that's left is worn out strings.

Yet rest can heal what strain destroys,
Renew the heart and flight with joys.
For even weary wings must find,
A gentle place to ease the mind.

49

Silent Saboteur

A shadow moved from perch to perch,
Whispering rumors, setting search.
"Watch your backs," the silence said,
"For not all friends fly straight ahead."

Trust dissolved like morning mist,
Loyalty grew harder to list.
The race had turned a darker twist,
A game of feathers, clenched in fists.

But light can pierce the darkest veil,
And truth will always find the trail.
Though shadows lurk, the brave will see,
A flock's true strength is unity.

50

Final Prep

Night fell quiet on the loft,
Wings tucked close, minds aloft.
Some prayed for strength, some prayed for luck,
All feeling nerves that tightly stuck.

The race was near no turning back,
The stage was set along the track.
And though the morning would be bright,
Dark fears lurked beneath the light.

But courage grows in silent night,
Preparing wings to claim their flight.
The dawn will test what hearts have sown,
And each must face the race alone.

51

False Start

A signal sounded—wings took flight,
But then a shout broke morning's light.
"False start! Return!" the coach decreed,
Chaos bloomed in frantic speed.

Pigeons flapped, then dropped, then paused,
Confusion swirling, none quite caused.
The race was more than just a run,
It was a test, a twisted fun.

Though false starts shake the bravest wings,
They teach the flock what patience brings.
To wait, to trust, to ready well,
Before the sound of final bell.

52

Overthinker's Regret

She counted beats, she counted breaths,
Analyzed all possible deaths.
In trying to plan every move,
She lost the will she'd tried to prove.

The race was wild, not neat or clear,
And fear held tightly, drawing near.
She wished for wings to fly on trust,
But doubt turned feathered flight to dust.

Yet in regret, a seed was sown,
To trust the flight, to stand alone.
For sometimes wings must leap and dive,
To feel alive, to truly thrive.

53

Crow's Cackle

A crow cawed loud from nearby tree,
Mocking pigeons' misery.
"Your race is folly, winged fools,
Bound to crash by foolish rules."

The flock ignored the blackened bird,
But inside, doubt grew like a word.
Was victory worth all the pain?
Or just a cycle spun in vain?

Still through the noise, the pigeons flew,
Some hearts were strong, some doubts they knew.
For every cackle, every jeer,
Only made their purpose clear.

54

Exhausted Alliance

Two pigeons perched, side by side,
Sharing tales of training's tide.
Exhausted, ragged, but still bound,
In shared despair, some hope was found.

"Together we might reach the end,"
They said, "Or find a way to mend."
For in a race that drains and frays,
Friendship lights the darkest days.

And so they flapped in tandem flight,
Against the endless, tiring fight.
For bonds like these can build a bridge,
To carry wings beyond the ridge.

55

Last Feed

The trough was empty, hunger grew,
But still they pecked as if they knew.
That fuel was more than just a bite,
It sparked the heart to chase the light.

Some ate fast, some ate in fear,
Each bite soaked with silent tear.
For strength was needed—this they knew,
To face the race they never chose.

Though empty bellies pressed their claim,
Their spirits burned a steady flame.
For hunger's fire can forge the strong,
To carry wings where dreams belong.

56

Whispered Worries

Late at night, the pigeons spoke,
Of dreams deferred and futures broke.
Whispers floated through the air,
Of fear and doubt and deep despair.

"Will it end?" one asked in hush,
"Or will we race till all is crushed?"
The loft replied with silent cold,
No answers given, only old.

Yet through the dark, a flicker grew,
A hope that whispered, faint but true.
That wings might one day rise and soar,
Beyond the fears they carried sore.

57

Flightless Trainer

The coach stood proud, but one could see,
He'd never truly flown free.
Wings too weak, his spirit torn,
Yet still he led each weary morn.

His words inspired, yet rang hollow,
A path too hard for those who follow.
He preached the race, but deep inside,
He envied those who dared to glide.

And though his flight was left behind,
His knowledge shaped each weary mind.
For even clipped wings can still guide,
If honesty and hope reside.

58

Perch of Pressure

Each pigeon sat upon a ledge,
Balanced close to the rooftop edge.
The crowd below, a noisy sea,
Urging them toward destiny.

But fear clung tight like winter's chill,
No wing can fly on fear and will.
The ledge was thin, the moment vast,
The race approached, coming fast.

Yet in the silence, deep inside,
A voice whispered to take the ride.
For courage grows when wings leap free,
And fear dissolves in bravery.

59

Feathers Shed

Some pigeons dropped their feathers loose,
In hope that lightness might reduce.
The weight of worry, stress, and doubt,
But loss made flying harder out.

For sometimes what we shed in pain,
Leaves gaps too wide to regain.
And lightness gained can bring its cost,
When parts of self are left and lost.

Still some believed the shedding's call,
Though what was lost could risk the fall.
For balance lies in what we keep,
Not just in what we cast to deep.

60

Last Training Flight

The sun rose low, the final drill,
Wings stretched out against the chill.
A nervous hush across the flock,
The quiet before the shock.

This flight would end the test and wait,
The day that brings the final gate.
Each pigeon braced, some prayed aloud,
Ready to soar, or fall in crowd.

No matter who would touch the sky,
Or who would falter, bleed, or try.
The journey's mark was in the flight,
The courage found within the fight.

PART 3: THE GREAT SKY DIVE

> “In the madness of the race, clarity is the hardest flight.”

61

False Confidence

Some strutted proud with chests outflared,
Their training tales loudly declared.
But inside nerves did twist and knot,
A shaky calm they all forgot.

Confidence, a fragile shell,
That cracks beneath the race's spell.
For pride can fade in just one flight,
And darkness swallow sudden light.

Yet even broken shells can mend,
And every fall brings chance to bend.
The bravest hearts still choose to try,
To face the truth beneath the sky.

62

Watchful Eyes

Eyes peered down from every ledge,
Judging each wing, each hopeful edge.
The loft was full of whispered doubt,
Who'd win? Who'd fall? Who'd give out?

The weight of watchers, heavy, near,
Made every flap a shout of fear.
And pigeons felt the pressing gaze,
That turned their dreams to cautious haze.

But in the silence, wings took flight,
Ignoring shadows, seeking light.
For courage grows beyond the stare,
When hearts decide they do not care.

63

Quiet Rebel

One bird refused the endless drill,
Said, "I won't run this pointless thrill."
She perched alone and looked around,
At chaos swirling all around.

No race to win, no prize to claim,
Just endless chase and endless game.
Her quiet stand, a silent plea,
To break the chain and just be free.

And though she flew a different way,
Her spirit soared beyond the fray.
For sometimes strength is found in pause,
A rebel's flight without a cause.

64

Last Night's Rest

Darkness wrapped the rooftop tight,
A final pause before the flight.
Some dreamed of victory's glow,
Others feared the race they'd know.

But sleep was fleeting, dreams were thin,
Tomorrow's race would soon begin.
And with the dawn, the wings would beat,
In frantic rush along the street.

Yet in that dark, a hope was sewn,
That every bird would find their own.
For rest can heal what fear has torn,
A promise kept beyond the morn.

65

Dawn's Breath

Light broke slow, a trembling hush,
The world prepared for morning's rush.
Pigeons stirred with nervous flight,
The race was now within their sight.

The rooftop held its breath, then sighed,
A moment poised before the tide.
The starting call was near, so near,
A race begun with hope and fear.

And as the sky began to glow,
Each wing would carve the winds to know.
That dawn itself is born from fight,
A fleeting chance to touch the light.

66

Starting Flap

A sudden flap, a piercing cry,
Wings burst forth into the sky.
The rooftop emptied, one by one,
Chasing dawn, chasing sun.

Hearts beat fast, beaks aimed high,
Clouds like mountains piled in the sky.
The race was on no turning back,
A wild, frantic feathered track.

With every flap the world expanded,
Boundaries broke and fears disbanded.
The journey started, bold and true,
A dance of wings in endless blue.

67

Gust's Betrayal

A gust blew fierce, unkind and sharp,
Tossing wings like ragged harp.
Some tumbled down, some veered off course,
Nature's whip, a ruthless force.

The sky was not a friendly place,
Each pigeon fought to keep its pace.
The race was more than strength and speed,
It demanded all, every need.

Yet through the storm, some found their way,
Learning how to bend and sway.
For power lies not just in might,
But in the will to hold on tight.

68

Midair Dance

Pigeons weaved in frantic flight,
Dodging shadows, chasing light.
A ballet wild, no music played,
Just flapping wings and breaths that stayed.

Collisions sparked, feathers flew,
Some soared high, some barely knew
If they'd survive the swirling fray,
Or fall behind, lose ground, give way.

Still through the chaos, rhythms formed,
A dance of life both wild and warmed.
Each wingbeat wrote its own refrain,
A song of struggle, loss, and gain.

69

Shiny Distraction

A glint caught eyes, a flash below,
A shiny coin in sun's bright glow.
Some veered off to snatch the prize,
Tempted by the sparkling lies.

But chasing gloss can cost the race,
And lead a wing to empty space.
For focus lost is ground betrayed,
A costly choice the wise forbade.

Yet lessons learned in sudden fall,
May teach the wisest of them all.
That treasures gleam but fleetingly,
True worth is found in constancy.

70

Panic Flap

A sudden cry, a frantic dive,
Chaos spread to every hive.
Wings crossed paths, a tumble spread,
Fear's sharp claws inside each head.

The race turned wild, a mad descent,
No plan survived the sudden event.
Yet still the pigeons pushed and flew,
For better hope or something new.

Amid the panic, courage grew,
A spark to light the darkness through.
For even fear can push to find,
A strength that's rooted in the mind.

71

Fallen Feather

A feather spiraled, lost to air,
Detached from wings with silent care.
It twirled and danced beyond the fight,
A lone ghost slipping out of sight.

The flock pressed on, none spared a glance,
Too caught within the frantic dance.
Yet that small loss, unnoticed, clear,
Whispered truths no one would hear.

For every flight leaves bits behind,
Small sacrifices intertwined.
The fallen things that go unseen,
Are part of what the race has been.

72

Broken Wing

One pigeon faltered, wing outstretched,
A sudden crack, a movement sketched.
Pain cut sharp through soaring flight,
Hope slipped away with fading light.

But still she flapped, refusing ground,
Though fear and hurt were tightly wound.
The race was more than just a game,
It was survival, not just fame.

Her spirit burned through aching pain,
A beacon lit in falling rain.
Proving strength's not just in speed,
But in the will to still proceed.

73

Shortcut Gamble

A daring few cut corners wide,
Slipping under rooftops' side.
Risking falls and sudden shocks,
To win the prize before the clocks.

Some soared on luck, some hit the wall,
Learning fast the race's call.
For shortcuts taken without care,
Can lead to crashes unaware.

Yet risk itself can carve new trails,
Where caution fears and courage sails.
And sometimes leaps beyond the line,
Are how the stars begin to shine.

74

Echoed Cheers

From distant ledges, voices rose,
Cheering on the highs and lows.
A chorus loud, a roaring sea,
Pushing wings to try and be.

Yet cheers can weigh as heavy chains,
Fueling hope, igniting pains.
The louder calls, the more they bind,
A tightening grip on mind.

Still in the noise, a bird can find,
A rhythm true, a peace of mind.
To rise above the crowd's loud voice,
And choose its own, untethered choice.

75

Midair Pause

For a moment, wings held still,
Above the chaos, over the thrill.
A breath suspended, time grew wide,
A fleeting calm in wild tide.

Then hearts resumed their frantic beat,
The race reclaimed in soaring heat.
No rest for wings that dare to dream,
In this mad, relentless stream.

Yet in that pause, a spark was lit,
A quiet strength to not submit.
For every breath between the flight,
Is where the soul renews its might.

76

Wind's Whispers

The wind, a sly and fickle friend,
Would push or pull or twist and bend.
Some pigeons caught its secret song,
While others drifted far too long.

A whispered breeze could change the game,
But none could predict its fickle aim.
The race was more than muscle and will,
It danced with air, unseen, until.

And in the end, the wisest knew,
The wind would choose what wings to woo.
A dance of chance both cruel and kind,
A fleeting breath to shape the mind.

77

Distant Glow

Far off, a light began to shine,
A beacon through the sky's design.
Some surged ahead, eyes fixed and bright,
Chasing promise in morning light.

But chasing glows can blind the wings,
And silence all the wiser things.
The closer sought, the more they yearned,
A prize elusive, never earned.

Yet still the glow can guide the way,
Through darkest night to break of day.
A hope that flickers, bright and thin,
A path that calls from deep within.

78

Midair Collision

Two wings crossed with sudden force,
Breaking rhythm, changing course.
Feathers flew like snow in spring,
Caught in chaos, hurtling.

Pain and fear sparked sharp and raw,
A cruel reminder of nature's law.
Yet from the crash, some found their flight,
Renewed with grit, restored with fight.

For sometimes broken things can heal,
And courage shapes what wounds reveal.
A fractured wing may still ascend,
A story only strength can mend.

79

Silent Watcher

A lone pigeon, quiet and still,
Observed the madness from the hill.
Not rushing, not falling behind,
But seeking peace within the mind.

The race below was loud and fast,
But sometimes slow wins at last.
For not all flights must chase the roar,
Some find strength in flying more.

And in her calm, the world would see,
A flight beyond urgency.
That steady wings can cross the sky,
Without the need to question why.

80

Sky's Reflection

The sky above was clear and vast,
Mirroring dreams too big to last.
Each wingbeat stirred the open air,
A fleeting hope, a whispered prayer.

And as they raced, they could not see,
The sky was both their chain and key.
In flying high, they touched the blue,
But wondered what was really true.

Perhaps the sky holds more than flight,
A space for dreams to burn so bright.
Yet grounded hearts may also find,
That truth can dwell in quiet mind.

81

Lost Wingmate

In the swirl of frantic flight,
One wingmate vanished from the sight.
Eyes searched skies, a silent plea,
But lost was lost in rivalry.

The race consumed both heart and mind,
Leaving kindness far behind.
Sometimes flying means to part,
A lonely journey, aching heart.

Yet in the loss, a seed may grow,
Of empathy that few may know.
That even when the wings divide,
The soul remains, forever tied.

82

Hollow Cheers

Cheers rose loud from distant roofs,
Echoes hollow, empty proofs.
Pigeons chased applause and fame,
But found the echoes all the same.

Noise that promised soaring flight,
Yet vanished in the dead of night.
For fleeting praise can't fill the soul,
It leaves a hole, a gaping hole.

True praise is quiet, deep, and known,
A seed within the heart that's grown.
Beyond the roar, beyond the crowd,
A voice that whispers clear and proud.

83

Reckless Dive

A pigeon dove with reckless speed,
Ignoring every warning heed.
The thrill was sharp, the risk was high,
But catching glory meant to fly.

Sometimes in madness, wings may break,
A price too steep for glory's sake.
Yet some will risk the fall or flight,
For chance, for dream, for fleeting light.

And though the fall may bring despair,
The courage shown is something rare.
For life is made of risks we take,
And flights we choose, despite the stakes.

84

Feathered Ghost

One bird slipped from the racing crowd,
Silent, fading, wrapped in cloud.
A shadow lost in endless blue,
A whisper of what once was true.

Not all who fly escape the cost,
Some dreams are gained, some dreams are lost.
The race is cruel, the sky is wide,
And wings may fail before the tide.

But every ghost leaves trails behind,
In memories and in the mind.
A silent song, a whispered name,
A flicker in the endless flame.

85

Turning Point

The skyline bent, the course was new,
A twist where only brave would flew.
The race was shifting no more clear,
Uncertainty replaced the cheer.

And in this moment, hearts did weigh,
If chasing on was the only way.
For sometimes races end before,
The finish line, the distant shore.

Yet choices made at turning tides,
Can lead to paths where strength abides.
The end's not always what we seek,
But where we learn the brave and meek.

86

Shattered Dream

A sudden gust, a broken wing,
Sent dreams crashing, shattering.
The sky once filled with hopeful cries,
Now echoed loss and muffled sighs.

Yet even shattered dreams can teach,
That strength is found beyond the breach.
For flight is more than winning's song,
It's rising up when all feels wrong.

From broken wings new hope can soar,
A chance to find what lies in store.
For every fall is but a start,
A stronger beat within the heart.

87

Silent Doubt

Between the flaps and frantic chase,
A silent doubt took quiet place.
A whispered thought, a shadowed fear,
Is this the path that's truly clear?

Yet voices drowned it in the roar,
Telling all to race once more.
But doubt, though small, can plant the seed,
Of questioning the race's need.

Sometimes the quiet voice inside,
Can lead the wings to turn and glide.
To find a path less worn, less tried,
Where true hearts dare to rest and bide.

88

Unexpected Ally

Amid the chaos, wings entwined,
Two strangers found their fates aligned.
A helping wing, a steady glide,
Shared strength against the rushing tide.

For sometimes in the fiercest storm,
A hand extended keeps hearts warm.
And racing alone can feel so cold,
But shared the race is brave and bold.

Together wings can rise and fall,
But bonded flight can break the wall.
In friendship's flight, the journey's sweet,
Two hearts that find the same beat.

89

False Finish

The skyline loomed, the end in sight,
But something wasn't quite right.
A false finish line appeared,
And hearts both leapt and dropped in fear.

The race was trickery in disguise,
Another test, another prize?
The journey stretched, the goal moved far,
A lesson harsh beneath the star.

Yet every twist and sudden turn,
Can teach what patience makes us learn.
That sometimes paths will shift and bend,
But every race still finds its end.

90

Breath Before

A moment paused, the world held tight,
Before the final burst of flight.
Wings rested briefly, chests did heave,
A breath to take, a chance to leave.

The race still called, the sky still wide,
But now the end was just in sight.
And every wing that dared to fly,
Carried hope beneath the sky.

With steady heart and sharpened gaze,
They launched anew into the haze.
For every end's a chance to start,
A race renewed within the heart.

PART 4: THE FINISH LINE

> “Sometimes the prize is just the weight we carry home.”

91

Final Surge

Wings pumped hard, a desperate cry,
The skyline looming, drawing nigh.
Every breath a fleeting fire,
Fueling one last, fierce desire.

The flock pressed on through wind and ache,
Each beat closer to the break.
Yet in the roar of final race,
Some lost their way, some found their place.

In this last stretch, the heart unfolds,
Revealing truths the race withholds.
For some the end means newfound grace,
For others, just the empty space.

92

Cracked Beak

A collision left a cracked beak,
Sharp pain that made the strong grow weak.
But still, the bird would not relent,
Pushed on through hurt, through discontent.

Sometimes strength is not in flight,
But in enduring the harshest night.
A silent will that breaks no sound,
Yet keeps the fallen off the ground.

The cracked beak tells a quiet tale,
Of battles fought beyond the pale.
A scar that marks the will to stand,
And fight despite a trembling hand.

93

Blind Chase

Eyes fixed forward, blind to all,
Ignoring signs, ignoring calls.
Chasing shadows, chasing light,
Lost inside the endless fight.

The prize seemed close, yet out of reach,
An unseen goal none dared breach.
A race not run with open eyes,
But driven by whispered lies.

Yet still the chase commands the flight,
Though reason fades beyond the sight.
For some must run through blinding haze,
To find their way through veiled maze.

94

Winged Doubt

A sudden pause in frantic race,
Doubt crept in, a shadowed face.
"What if this flight is all for naught?
What if the prize can't be caught?"

Yet voices drowned the quiet plea,
"Keep racing on, don't you see?"
But still, the seed of question grew,
A whisper breaking through the blue.

Within that seed, a spark might grow,
To challenge winds that push and blow.
A softer strength begins to rise,
The courage found in honest skies.

95

Broken Chain

A pigeon faltered, then broke free,
From chains unseen, invisibly.
The race still raged, but one took flight,
Away from shadows into light.

Sometimes the end's not just to win,
But to escape the race within.
To find a sky beyond the fight,
And claim a new, uncharted flight.

The broken chain leaves space to breathe,
A chance to live, to dream, to weave.
A path where wings can spread and glide,
No longer bound by fear or pride.

96

Flicker of Hope

Amid the storm, a flicker gleamed,
A fragile hope, or so it seemed.
Wings still beating, hearts still high,
Reaching for a distant sky.

But hope can blind as much as guide,
When caught within the roaring tide.
A light that leads, but also blinds,
The tangled path that racing winds.

Yet in that flicker, life is sewn,
A gentle thread of the unknown.
For even faintest sparks can burn,
And teach the wings which way to turn.

97

Tangled Flight

Wings collided, feathers torn,
Dreams entangled, spirits worn.
The dance of chaos, sharp and wild,
Bitter rage of dreams defiled.

Yet even in the tangled mess,
A spark of fierce tenacity's dress.
For broken wings still learn to soar,
And battered hearts still seek for more.

From frayed flight's edge, new strength is born,
A stubborn will that braves the storm.
The chaos fuels the drive inside,
A restless heart that won't subside.

98

Shadowed Leader

A pigeon led with shining gleam,
A hero born from fleeting dream.
But shadows trailed behind the crown,
Silent whispers pulling down.

For leadership can weigh like stone,
A lonely flight, a path unknown.
Behind the cheers and soaring praise,
Lie hidden costs and weary days.

Yet in the shadows grows a light,
A choice to rise and stand the fight.
For leaders brave the harshest skies,
Though burdened by unseen goodbyes.

99

Midair Whisper

Between the chaos, soft and low,
A whispered truth began to grow.
"Is this the race we truly choose?
Or just the one we never lose?"

But noise returned to drown the voice,
The racing heart, the frantic choice.
Yet still the whisper softly spoke,
A question in the racing smoke.

That whisper calls for something new,
A flight beyond the known and true.
A quiet hope to break the chain,
And find what lies beyond the pain.

100

Final Push

The skyline stretched, the end was near,
Exhaustion mixed with rising fear.
Every wingbeat harder fought,
For fleeting glory, dearly bought.

And in that push, a moment's grace,
The race became a frantic chase.
Not for prize or fame or cheer,
But just to finish, to persevere.

In final breath, the truth is clear:
It's not the end but what draws near.
A chance to rest, to heal, to find,
The peace long lost within the mind.

101

Silent Fall

A pigeon faltered, slipped from sight,
Plunged from grace in fading light.
No cheers, no cries just quiet air,
A silent fall from desperate dare.

Yet falling isn't always loss,
Sometimes a break, a needed pause.
To find new wings beyond the fall,
And rise again beyond the call.

The silent fall can mark a start,
A freeing of the weary heart.
For not all flights are straight and true,
Sometimes you fall to fly anew.

102

Flickering Flame

The fire within began to wane,
Burned low beneath the pounding strain.
The chase once fierce, now dim and frail,
A whispered doubt, a fragile veil.

But even flickers hold a spark,
To light the way through darkest dark.
And in that glow, a chance to see,
What truly fuels the flight to be.

That fragile flame may guide the lost,
A beacon worth the deepest cost.
For in the dimmest light is found,
The strength to stand, to leave the ground.

103

Empty Crowd

The rooftops echoed empty cheers,
Hollow praise for racing peers.
The crowd had gathered, yet stood still,
Watching wings bend to the will.

For applause can fade like fleeting song,
And crowds forget where hearts belong.
A fleeting rush, a passing thrill,
That leaves the soul to climb uphill.

Behind the noise, a silence grows,
Where true belonging seldom shows.
And wings that fly beyond the crowd,
Are free from praise and hollow loud.

104

Worn Feather

A single feather, worn and bent,
Told tales of battles never spent.
A symbol not of victory won,
But of the miles in endless run.

For glory's weight can bend the proud,
And silence dreams once spoken loud.
Yet worn feathers hold quiet grace,
The marks of every hard-fought race.

Each bend and tear, a story told,
Of courage born through trials bold.
A quiet badge of honor's cost,
Of paths endured and never lost.

105

Quiet Question

Amid the rush, a question rose,
Soft as breeze, beneath the throes:
"Why do we chase the distant light,
When stars above shine calm and bright?"

No answer came from frantic flight,
Just racing hearts in endless night.
But still the question gently stayed,
A whisper in the skies betrayed.

This quiet thought may find a home,
In hearts that dare to cease to roam.
To seek beyond the constant race,
A truer sky, a kinder place.

106

Hollow Prize

The finish line came into view,
A shining mark, a fading hue.
But what was once a hoped for prize,
Now seemed to dim before their eyes.

An empty perch, a vacant throne,
A crown of feathers, made of stone.
The glory lost its luster bright,
Revealed the hollow in the light.

What once was chased with all their might,
Now fades into the failing light.
A lesson writ in wings and pain,
That not all gains are truly gains.

107

Quiet After

Silence settled on the roof,
The race had ended what was proof?
The cheers dissolved into the air,
Leaving echoes cold and bare.

Pigeons paused, wings tired and worn,
Reflecting on what they'd borne.
The cost of chasing distant dreams,
More bitter than it first had seemed.

Yet in the hush, a chance to heal,
To let the wounds begin to seal.
And from the quiet, soft and deep,
New hopes and dreams begin to leap.

108

Weight of Wings

Heavy wings and heavier hearts,
Bearing scars from all the starts.
The race was more than simple flight,
A burden carried out of sight.

Each feather told a secret pain,
Of sacrifice and loss in vain.
The flight for glory, bright and high,
Had drained the soul, left wings to cry.

But even weighed and bruised and worn,
The wings can rise to greet the morn.
For strength is born in pain endured,
And hope in hearts long reassured.

109

Crowd's Whisper

From the loft, the crowd still spoke,
In words that stung and gently poked.
"Run faster, fly higher still,
Success is not a matter of will?"

But pigeons knew the truth behind,
A race not theirs, but all combined.
A pressure from the gathered throng,
That pushed them all to chase the wrong.

And so they seek a different tune,
Beyond the crowd, beyond the moon.
To fly not for the crowd's loud cheer,
But for a sky that feels sincere.

110

Feather's Fall

One feather slipped from tired wing,
Drifting slow, a silent thing.
It floated down, away from race,
A symbol lost in empty space.

Sometimes letting go is strength,
Not measured in the distance length.
A gentle fall to find the ground,
Where peace and quiet might be found.

And in that fall, a soft release,
A moment's pause, a quiet peace.
For sometimes flight begins anew,
When burdens shed come into view.

111

Unseen Chains

Invisible, yet tightly bound,
By unseen chains, the race was crowned.
The pigeons ran but did not choose,
Caught in webs they could not lose.

A gilded cage of whispered rules,
Where freedom hid behind the duels.
The loft's promises bright and thin,
Masked the cost locked deep within.

But breaking chains, though frail and slight,
Can lead the wings toward the light.
And freedom's song, once softly heard,
Becomes the flight beyond the herd.

112

Last Glance

Before departing from the race,
A pigeon took a backward glance.
At rooftops blurred, the endless flight,
The moments lost within the fight.

A fleeting thought of what could be,
A life beyond the sky and spree.
The choice to soar or ground the wing,
A question only silence brings.

That final glance may spark a flame,
To seek a life beyond the game.
To find a sky not marked by pain,
And fly unbound, beyond the chain.

113

Flock's Weight

Together yet alone they stood,
Each bearing burdens none could good.
The weight of flock and fleeting fame,
A silent, shared, relentless game.

In unity, the pressure grew,
An unseen force that none withdrew.
For in the race they all were caught,
By hope, by fear, by lessons taught.

Yet in the weight, a strength is born,
From shared struggles, new paths worn.
For none must fly the race alone,
Together, wings can find new home.

114

Shattered Mirror

The prize once mirrored shining dreams,
Reflected hopes and future schemes.
But cracks appeared upon the glass,
Distorting what had come to pass.

What once was clear was now askew,
The race exposed its false debut.
And in the shards, the pigeons saw,
The cost of chasing hollow law.

But in the fragments, truth may gleam,
A chance to heal the broken dream.
To piece together what remains,
A flight beyond the glass's chains.

115

Quiet Flight

Some chose silence after the race,
A quiet flight, a slower pace.
Away from noise, away from strife,
Seeking calm beyond the life.

Not every wing must chase the sky,
Some find peace in simply fly.
And in the stillness, soft and light,
They find the strength to reignite.

For in the quiet, wings are free,
To write new tales of what can be.
A gentle flight, a softer song,
The place where tired hearts belong.

116

Last Race

The race is done, but echoes stay,
In hearts that ran, then lost their way.
Not all returned with wings intact,
Some found themselves in faded fact.

Yet even in the final flight,
There's room to dream beyond the night.
For every end, a new start waits,
Beyond the rooftops, past the gates.

And so the wings prepare to soar,
To seek what life has held in store.
For endings bring beginnings near,
New skies ahead, horizons clear.

117

Unwritten Sky

Beyond the finish, skies unfold,
Stories new and yet untold.
No course charted, no prize to claim,
Just open air, no need for fame.

A canvas vast, untouched, unknown,
Where pigeons fly on paths their own.
Free from race, free from the cost,
In newfound flight, nothing's lost.

Each wingbeat writes a tale anew,
Of journeys chosen, skies in view.
The unwritten sky invites the bold,
To chase the dreams not bought or sold.

118

Feather's Path

That fallen feather, soft and light,
Drifted onward, out of sight.
A symbol not of loss or shame,
But of the courage to reclaim.

To choose the path not paved or worn,
To fly by heart, not by the scorn.
A gentle journey, slow and true,
The flight that's always just for you.

Along that path, new winds may call,
And lead the wings beyond the fall.
A softer journey, brave and kind,
The feather's path, a flight defined.

119

Silent Promise

A promise made without a word,
In silent wings and hope deferred.
That freedom lies not in the chase,
But in the quiet, open space.

Where pigeons soar beyond the roar,
And find their own sky to explore.
No longer bound by crowded cries,
Just endless blue and open skies.

This silent vow sustains the flight,
A guiding star beyond the night.
A hope that softly lights the way,
To dawn of peace, a freer day.

120

New Dawn

The dawn breaks soft on rooftops wide,
A new day calls with gentle tide.
No more the race, no more the strain,
Just skies to fly and dreams to gain.

The pigeons rise with quiet grace,
Each finding now their own true place.
In peace, in flight, beyond the race,
A world reborn, a freer space.

And in that dawn, a future gleams,
A sky alive with endless dreams.
The race is past, the wings are new,
The flight ahead, forever true.

9 789334 316223

Printed at Repro India Ltd.